Bustle & Sew Magazine
October 2012

HELEN DICKSON

Issue 21 of the independent, quirky
stitching e-zine now available in print for
you to enjoy

Bustle & Sew
www.bustleandsew.com

A Bustle & Sew Publication

Copyright © Bustle & Sew Limited 2012

The right of Helen Dickson to be identified as the author of this work has been asserted in accordance with the Copyright, Designs and Patents Act 1988.

ISBN-13: 978-1479393046

ISBN-10: 1479393045

First published 2012 by:
Bustle & Sew
Coombe Leigh
Chillington
Kingsbridge
Devon TQ7 2LE
UK

www.bustleandsew.com

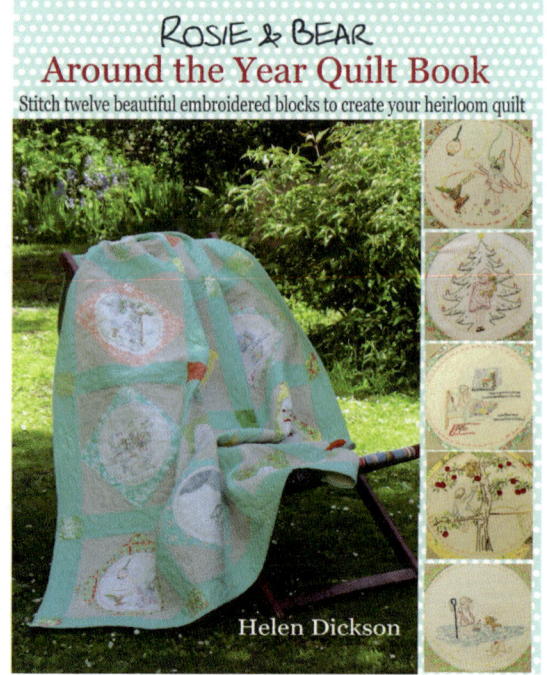

Available in print from Amazon worldwide or download as a pdf file from the Bustle & Sew website

http:bustleandsew.com

Best value for back issues: purchase Bundle 3 (issues 13 to 18) on the Bustle & Sew website and receive free bonus CD to back up your collection (pay for p&p only).

http://bustleandsew.com/magazine

Hello,

and welcome to the 21st issue of the Bustle & Sew ezine.

October is the month that I begin to plan my Christmas stitching, and this is reflected in this month's issue. Inside you'll discover my Baby Owls Advent Calendar, "I Saw Three Ships" table runner and "Star of Wonder" Rosie & Bear embroidery. October isn't all about Christmas though, and you'll also discover my Blackbird Patchwork Cushion Cover, Swan Softies and a great little Stitchery from SewFlapdoodle – "Halloween Fun".

Autumn berries in the hedgerow

There's also an interview with Pipany, a very talented creator from Cornwall, England, articles, reviews and features, as well as (I am sorry to say) the very last Rosie's Recipes. Rosie is thrilled and delighted to be starting an exciting new job in October. Her travelling time will be longer which means that sadly she won't have time to contribute on a regular basis any more. I am hoping to persuade her to return with some "specials" from time to time though and I'm sure you'll join me in wishing her all the best in her new job.

I hope you enjoy this month's issue and don't forget to go crunching through the leaves – just as Ben and I love to do …. have a wonderful October wherever you are.

Best wishes

Helen xx

Contents:

Baby Owls Advent Calendar

These baby owls have all hung up their Christmas stockings in the hope that Santa will remember them this Christmas Eve.

Deceptively easy project featuring freestyle machine embroidery - the stockings are stitched and then cut out. Then simply peg them to the calendar with those miniature clothes pegs you use for hanging cards. Finished calendar measures 19" x 26".

You will need:

- 19 x 26 ¼" piece of medium weight navy blue fabric
- 19 x 26" piece of light-weight batting
- 19 x 7 ¼" piece of medium weight brown check fabric
- 20" x 6" piece of brown felt for tree (if you have a shorter, fatter piece this is fine, you can join it in the middle and stitch over the join).
- 1 FQ red polka dot fabric for stockings
- 24" square red felt for backing stockings
- 12" x 6" cream/blue polka dot fabric for stocking tops
- Assorted scraps of fabric in browns, creams and other natural colours for the owls' bodies
- Assorted scraps of fabric in greens for leaves
- 5" square gold fabric for star
- 6" square of beige felt for eyes
- 4" square aqua blue fabric for eyes
- Small amount yellow felt for beaks and matching floss for stitching feet.
- 7 pairs of ¼" buttons for eyes
- 2 ½ yards baker's twine, needle it will fit through
- 3 yards bias binding
- 1" curtain rings for hanging
- 24 (or 25 if preferred) small pegs - the sort you can purchase for hanging cards.
- 8" square white cotton fabric suitable for printing numbers on. *(Either use your printer, or write with a fabric marker, or use a stamp to mark the numbers. If you're using a printer, then I have provided the numbers I used later in the pattern.)*
- Darning/embroidery foot for your sewing machine.

- Black, cream and navy thread for your needle
- Bondaweb or fabric adhesive
- Temporary fabric marker pen

Background and Tree:

- Join your navy and blue fabrics along one 19" edge using a ¼" seam allowance. Press seam open.
- Trace tree shapes onto Bondaweb using the template on the next page. You will need to resize this template - the tree measures 19" tall from top to bottom, or simply cut the shapes freehand using the template image as a guide. Do not cut straight lines - the tree limbs should be gently curving and organic with rounded ends.
- Position your tree on the background, centering it horizontally. The base of the trunk should be 1 ½" up from the bottom of the background panel.
- Underlap the branches with the trunk as shown by the dotted lines on the template so there are no gaps.
- When you're happy with the positioning iron into place.
- With black thread in your machine needle and a lighter colour in your bobbin (this will give a less harsh effect) stitch twice around the edges of the tree trunk and branches. You are aiming for a scribbled effect - don't be too neat. If you like, you could also include a few knots and twirls as you stitch as shown in the image below:

Tree template. Cut branches separately and
overlap with trunk as shown by dotted lines.
Tree measures 19" from bottom of trunk to
its tip.

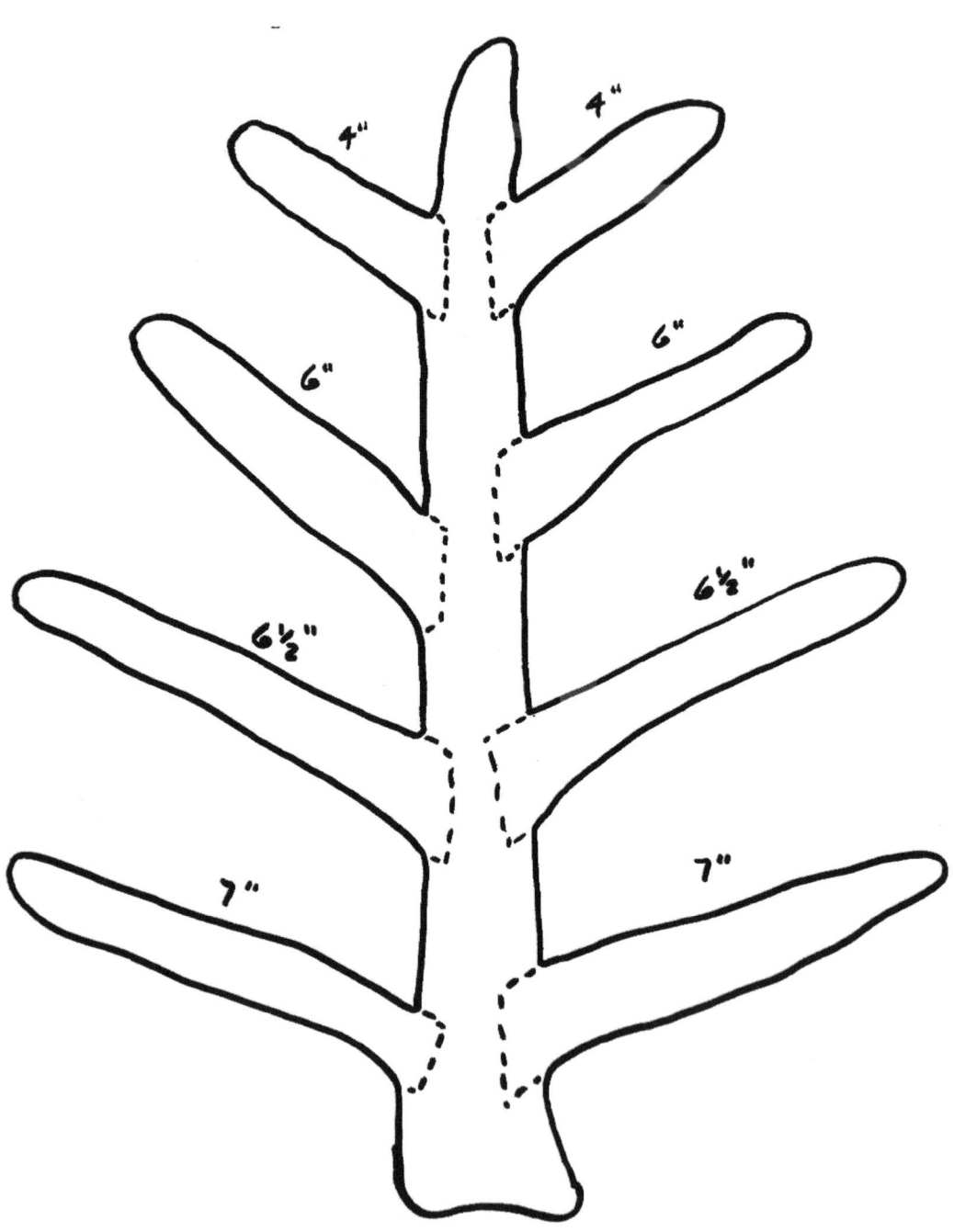

- Now trace onto Bondaweb, fuse to your green fabrics, and cut out 24 simple leaf shapes (see photograph for guidance.

- Position these leaves at the end of the branches, again using the photograph as guidance for positioning (there is no right and wrong!).

- When you're happy with the positioning iron into place, then machine stitch as shown below, going twice around the edge and then up into the middle and back to look like the centre vein of the leaf.

- Press lightly on the back then place to one side for the time being.

Make your owls:

- Using the template, trace the shapes onto Bondaweb. You may need to re-size the template - each owl should measure 3" tall.

- Then cut 7 owl bodies from your brown fabrics, 7 chests from cream, 7 beige felt spectacles and 14 aqua eyes.

- Position owls on branches using the photograph at the beginning of this pattern as a guide. Start with the bodies, then chests, spectacles and eyes. The spectacles overlap the chests as shown by the dotted line on the template.

- When you're happy with the positioning of your owls fuse them into place by ironing and machine stitch as before.

Owl measures 3" high

- Add small triangles of yellow felt for beaks, then machine stitch your owls to the background panel.

- Stitch buttons to eyes with black floss, and indicate feet with a few straight stitches in yellow floss.

Make your stockings:

- Make a sandwich from red felt, Bondaweb and red polka dot fabric, ironing them together.

- Then draw around your stocking template (see next page) 24 or 25 times using your temporary fabric marker pen

Your stocking template should measure 5 high. Reverse some of the stockings so they will hang in opposite directions.

- Print onto fabric and cut out the numbers for your stockings (or cut circles of white fabric and stamp or write the numbers on to them). Fuse numbers to stockings.

- Fuse Bondaweb onto the reverse of your cream and blue dotty fabric, then trace and cut out 24 or 25 stocking tops.

- Fuse stocking tops to stockings

- Now, with your darning foot and black thread in your needle machine stitch twice around edge of stocking just inside the lines you drew around the template. Make a few extra lines to indicate toe and heel of stocking and go around cream and blue dotty stocking top twice as well. Go around the numbers once. It's much easier to stitch such small pieces before you cut them out!

- Cut your stockings out. If any of the lines you drew can be seen then remove them with water or wait for them to fade (depending on the type of marker pen you used).

- Press lightly on reverse.

- Place to one side for the moment.

Assemble your calendar:

- Make a sandwich from your backing fabric (right side down), batting and calendar front (right side up) and pin or tack together.

- With navy thread in your needle and your darning foot, quilt around the edge of the tree, leaves and owl, changing the thread in your needle to brown when you quilt around the base of the tree.

- Bind the edges of your calendar with your bias binding.

- Now you're going to add your baker's twine to the branches to hang the stockings from.

- Cut a 15" length of twine and thread it into your needle and push it through the front of your quilted calendar right to the back, leaving most of it at the front.

- Unthread your needle and make a knot in the twine.

- Thread your needle again and push through at the other end of the branch again securing with a knot at the back.

8

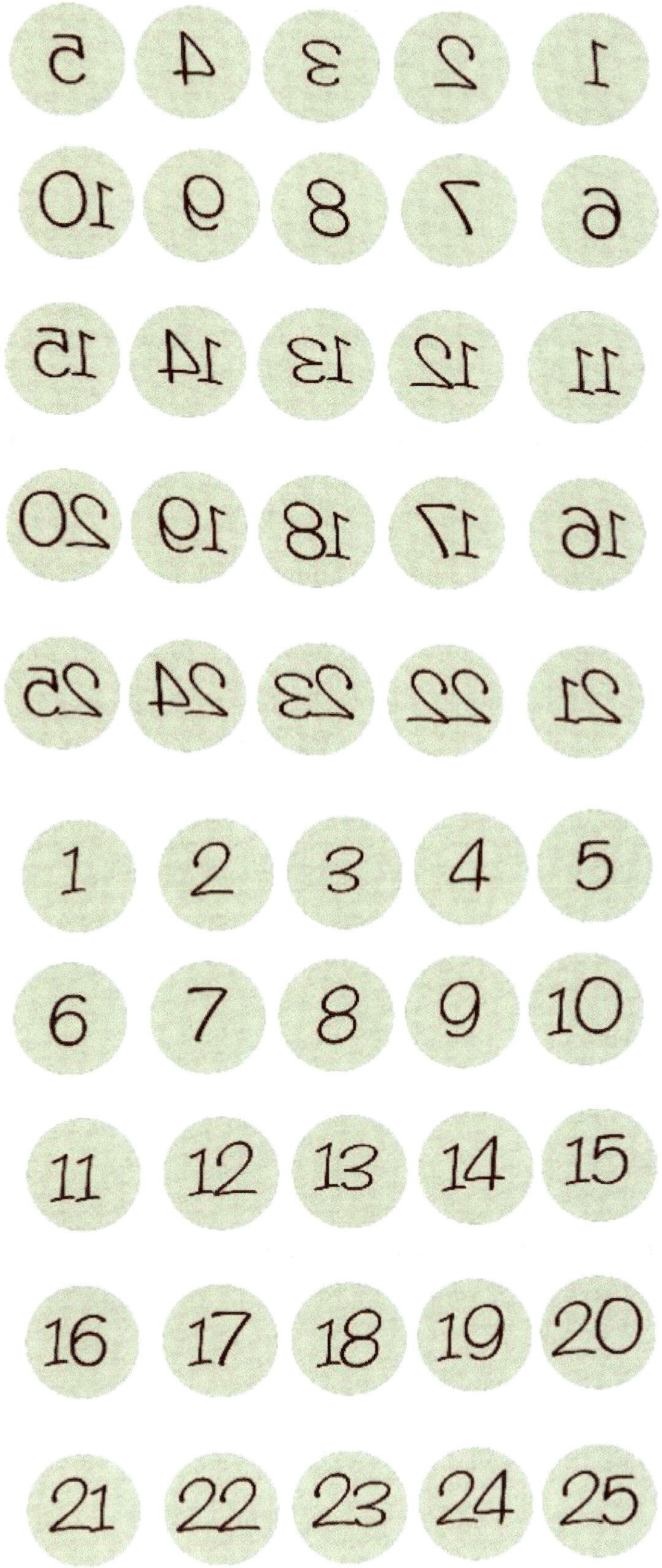
1 2 3 4 5
6 7 8 9 10
11 12 13 14 15
16 17 18 19 20
21 22 23 24 25

- Repeat for all the branches.
- Trim the tails of twine as shown in the image below.

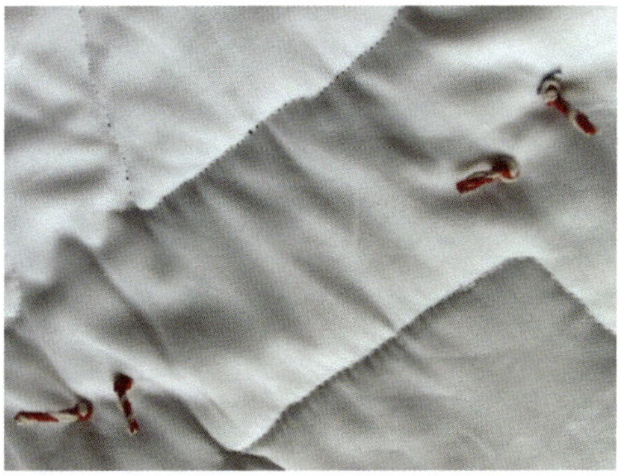

- Stitch the two curtain rings to the back for hanging (or you could use a quilt hanger if preferred,)
- Peg your stockings to the twine with the miniature pegs - one each day until Christmas!

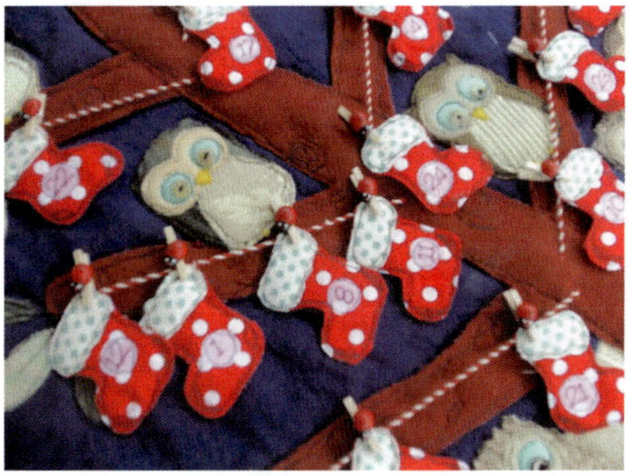

FINISHED!!

Caring for your Vintage Fabrics

Some advice on keeping your vintage fabrics in the best possible condition - ready for that very special project ......

Calendar Bunnies Quilt
A mixture of vintage and modern fabrics.

If you're a regular reader of the Bustle & Sew e-zine, or have purchased my patterns then you'll already know that I love to source and use vintage fabrics in my designs. These range from elderly moth-eaten blankets, to damaged, unloved and discarded cashmere and woollen garments (great for felting) and all kinds of tweeds, cottons, linens - indeed any sort of natural fibre I can get my hands on.

I'm not a great fan of manmade fibres, finding them far less rewarding to work with, but will occasionally accept a polyester-cotton blend.

I'm a bit of a fabric-addict I'm afraid, and as well as sourcing online I love to rummage through the rails of our local charity/thrift stores looking for unusual fabrics that can be re-purposed into Bustle & Sew designs. I have cupboards and boxes full of my finds, so that I will never run out(!) and almost always have the right piece of fabric for a particular new

inspiration. It's important to look beyond the faded, tattered (or even smelly) garment or remnant to view its potential when unpicked, sliced up, washed and remade into a new project.

Don't discount that gentleman's tweed jacket with the pocket half-ripped off, moth holes in the sleeves and missing most of its buttons - tweed is the most wonderful fabric for a whole range of projects - working particularly well when used for animals in freestyle machine embroidery.

Don't discard even the smallest scraps of fabric - my "I Saw Three Ships" applique table runner uses the very smallest of pieces. Some are less than 1" square and it's the variety of fabrics that make it special - and of course unique - nobody else will have just the same selection as you.

Detail from "I Saw Three Ships"

Some of the scraps I use are less than 1" square. The boat is cut from a (beyond repair) tweed jacket

Understanding your fabrics and how to restore and revive them is key to using vintage fabrics successfully, and the following tips from Nan Jaeger of Revival Fabrics are well worth following, especially if you're planning to store your treasures for any length of time:

Nan's Top 36 Tips:

Vintage fabric care is important. As fabric collectors know, the better the condition, the more valuable a vintage fabric. How fabric is stored, cared for, cleaned, and ironed will determine the value and usability over time.

Yet many collectors end up sad and disappointed after lovingly unfolding a cherished vintage quilting cotton to discover irreversible mould spots, expensive silk that shatters with merely the touch of the hand, and feel emotionally crushed like the permanently flattened nap of ironed wool.

Storing your Fabrics

Properly stored and cared for, the value of vintage fabrics will go up over time and can be used for garments and quilting years from now.

Coastguard Cottages

A mixture of vintage and modern fabrics

- Make sure fabrics are dust-free and clean before storing. Place nylons over a vacuum nozzle and gently vacuum dust from fabric.

- Store fabrics at room temperature in a dark area such as a closet.

- Do not store vintage fabrics in damp basements or hot attics.

- 65 - 70 degrees is an ideal room temperature. Humidity should be about 82 percent.

- Roll fabric instead of folding, to prevent stressed fibers at creases.

Pincushion Mice

Crafted from vintage blanket and felted cashmere. Note the feedsack fabrics displayed on old wooden cotton reels.

- If fabrics are stored folded, periodically refold to prevent dust settling in creases.

- Drape unbleached 100% cotton over fabric and hang on a padded hanger.

- Do not store fabrics against wood. Place unbleached muslin or acid tissue as a barrier between the fabric and wood to prevent spots from oil in the wood.

- Don't store fabric in tightly enclosed plastic boxes and bags. Fabric needs air circulation to prevent condensation and mould growth.

- Store vintage fabrics in acid-free boxes with acid-free tissue placed between fabrics.

- Use dried lavender instead of mothballs to repel insects naturally, without chemicals.

*Vintage fabrics are great for applique work
Detail from "Fairy Tale in Blue"*

Clean Vintage Fabrics Like Grandma

It's best to buy vintage fabrics in mint, unused condition. You'll avoid the hassle of washing, and the fabric is more valuable. However, sometimes a vintage fabric found with only a minor spot can be salvaged with proper cleaning.

Take great care when cleaning vintage fabric. Chemicals in the cleaners on the grocery shelves today may not be compatible with the dyes that were used to print vintage fabrics. Use the wrong cleaner and the dye may run in some vintage fabrics.

To avoid faded and fabrics stripped of their colour, clean fabrics from Grandma's time as Grandma did. She washed garments and fabrics by hand, and didn't use a dryer but instead laid textiles flat to dry or hung on a line. We don't have all of the same cleaners as Grandma; use proper substitutes.

- Make sure your chosen professional cleaner or dry cleaner is experienced with old textiles. Ask a textile conservator, quilt shop, or art museum to recommend professional cleaners.

- Test a small piece for colour-fastness before cleaning the whole fabric.

- Wear rubber gloves while handling fabric and chemicals.

- Do not wash vintage Fiberglass fabrics in the washing machine. Fine pieces of glass will be in your next load. Wear gloves when handling wet Fiberglass, hand wash, and lay flat to dry.

- Rust stains may come out with a paste of salt and white vinegar.

- Avoid the use of fabric softener and fabric softener sheets. Both can leave residue behind.

- Don't use hairspray as a stain remover. Hairspray may stain, especially silk fabric.

- Gently squeeze, not wring, water out. Blot dry with a towel and lay flat to dry on a clean surface.

- It's good practice to professionally clean silk, rayon, and home decorating weight fabrics.

- Handle wet vintage rayon fabric with care. Professional cleaning is advised.

*Charlie the Patchwork Elephant uses
vintage feedsack pieces*

- Vintage and antique chintz fabrics may lose original glaze if washed. Professional cleaning is recommended.

Iron in Haste and Your Vintage Fabrics will go to Waste

Iron incorrectly and a pristine vintage fabric may well turn into your next limp and useless rag. Often ironing mistakes cause damage to fabric that is irreversible.

Carefully ironed, Retro polyester won't turn into a crunchy melted mess and unsightly shine marks won't spoil valuable vintage rayon fabric. To maintain the valuable original condition of all vintage fabrics, take the correct precautions when ironing.

- Set iron to the correct temperature.

- Clean your hands before handling fabric.

- Do not iron dirty or stained vintage fabrics. Stains may set permanently.

- To avoid clogs, use distilled water in your iron.
  o To prevent iron scorch marks use a well-padded ironing board.

- Dry iron silk to prevent watermarks.

- Iron linen slightly damp. Wrinkles smooth out easily.

- Use caution when ironing with starch. Hot, scorched starch may transfer on to the fabric.

- Iron the reverse of fabrics. Vintage fabrics with dark backgrounds are prone to show iron marks.

- To restore chintz and polished cotton glaze, place wax paper face down on the fabric and iron the non-wax side of the wax paper.

- If vintage flannel fabric has pills, pick the largest pills off by hand, and iron nap flat.

- Steam wool. Do not iron.

- Steam, do not iron velvet.

- Hang velvet fabric near a hot shower to steam out wrinkles. Or, use the steam setting of an iron, steam the reverse, and brush the velvet nap. At an even pace, run steam up and down. Don't let the steam rest in one spot for long.

- Don't directly iron Retro fabrics such as polyester. Place a pillowcase on the fabric, and then iron.

Alphabet Animals is another Bustle & Sew design that uses vintage fabrics - this time feedsack, old shirt fabric, and even some vintage buttons for the letters "I" and "Z"!

36 tips from Nan Jaeger of Revival Fabrics.

http://www.revivalfabrics.com

© 2008. Reproduced with permission.

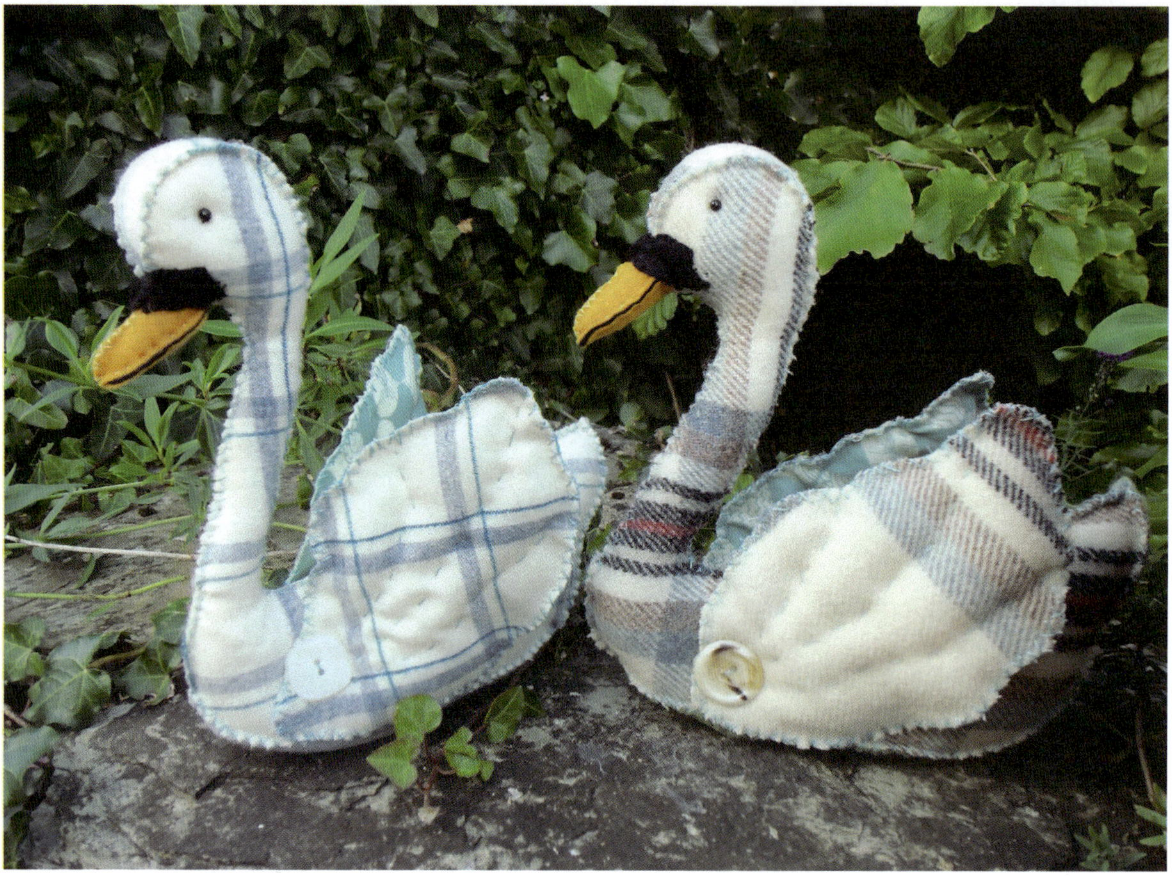

Swan Softie Pattern

These little swans measure 9" tall and are a great way to use vintage blanket or felt pieces. They are not intended to be given to children as toys.

They're probably not a beginner's project, but if you have some experience of softie making then you'll discover that they take more time and patience than skill. There is some simple wiring - just a single piece to support the neck.

You will need:

- 14" x 20" piece of felt, woollen fabric or old blanket (must be non-stretchy and not easy to fray)
- 8" x 10" contrast fabric for insides of wings
- 10" x 3" felt for base (or alternatively cut from your large piece of felt, there will be enough)
- Scraps of orange and black felt
- 12" garden wire
- 2 x 1" buttons for base of wings
- 2 x ⅛ " shiny black beads for eyes
- Black and orange cotton floss
- Floss to harmonise with the colours of your fabric (for stitching seams)
- Round pebble (about 2" long)
- Medium weight card
- Good quality toy stuffing
- Stuffing stick *
- Curved needle & long (eg sashiko needle)

Method:

- Cut out your pieces from the template on the following pages. To fit the page size he template is given slightly smaller than the size swan I made, but I have included the exact measurements of two of the pieces to enable you to resize if you wish. Of course you can make a smaller (or indeed larger!) swan if you wish.

- The pieces are joined by placing right sides together and working over the edges with cross stitch in 2 strands of floss. Work half-cross stitches in one direction first, then return and complete the stitch in the other direction. This gives your seam added strength as if the thread breaks in one place, it won't completely unravel.

- First join the head gusset to the body pieces, working from A to B on both sides.

- Now join the top seam from B to C and then the under-body piece on both sides from C to D, leaving a gap for stuffing as shown.

- Join beneath beak from X to Z

- Take your piece of wire and bend it into a loop at both ends. You can bind with tape if preferred but I didn't do this.

- Bend your wire to the shape of the neck as shown by the dotted line on the template

- Stuff the top of the head and add stuffing to the back of the neck, then insert the wire so that it extends into the body and head as shown on the template.

- Stuff your head firmly around the wire (use your stuffing stick*) with small pieces of stuffing - if you add large pieces your head will become lumpy.

- Continue stuffing down into the neck, making sure the wire is firmly embedded in the stuffing and that you have no lumps. Sew from X to Y as you stuff. Use half cross stitch as before, returning to complete the stitch when the neck is finished.

- Part stuff body, then insert pebble to give swan stability. Surround pebble with stuffing and then insert your card base to give your swan a nice flat firm bottom to stand on.

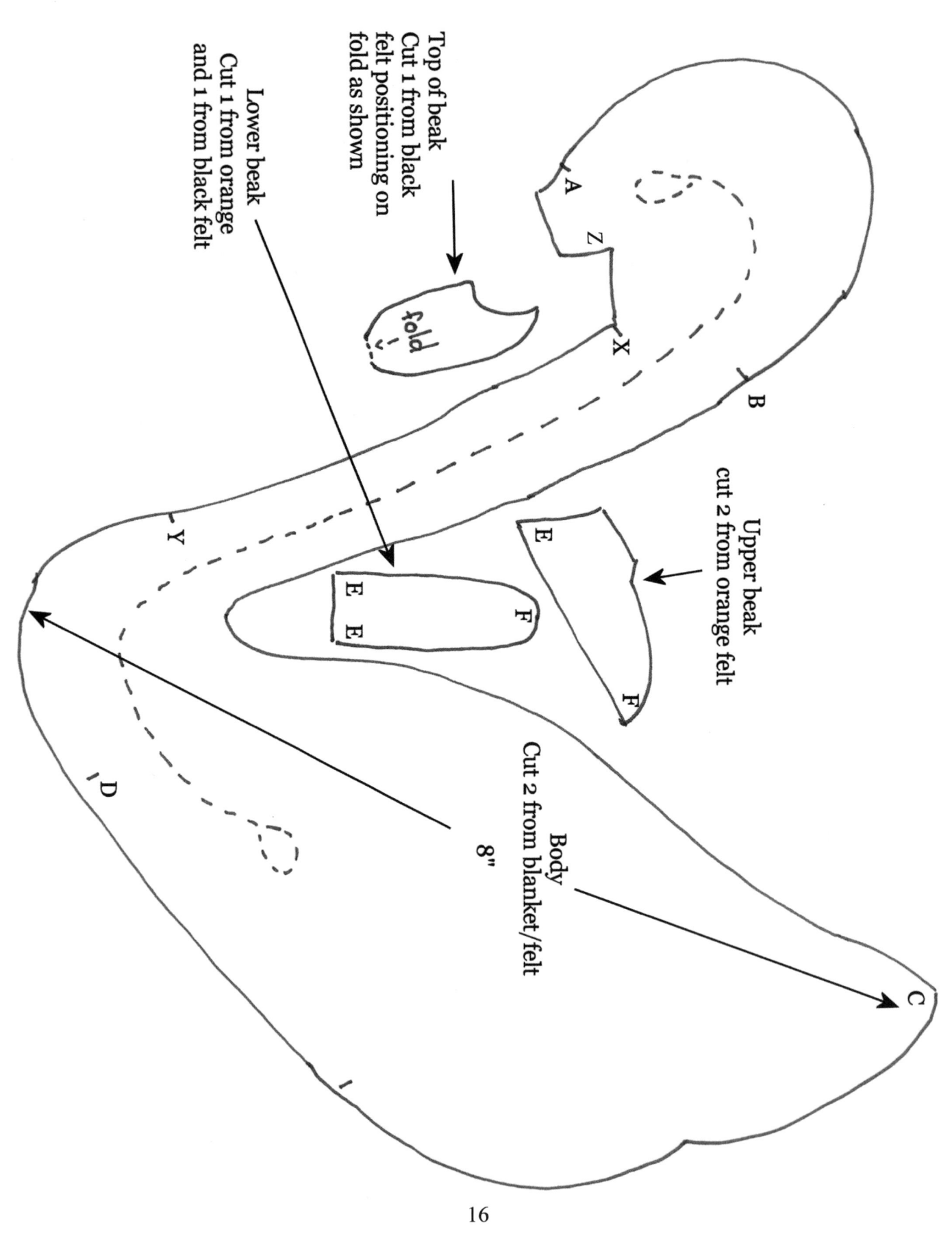

Top of beak
Cut 1 from black
felt positioning on
fold as shown

fold

Lower beak
Cut 1 from orange
and 1 from black felt

A

Z

X

B

Upper beak
cut 2 from orange felt

E

E

E

F

E

F

Y

Body
Cut 2 from blanket/felt

8"

D

C

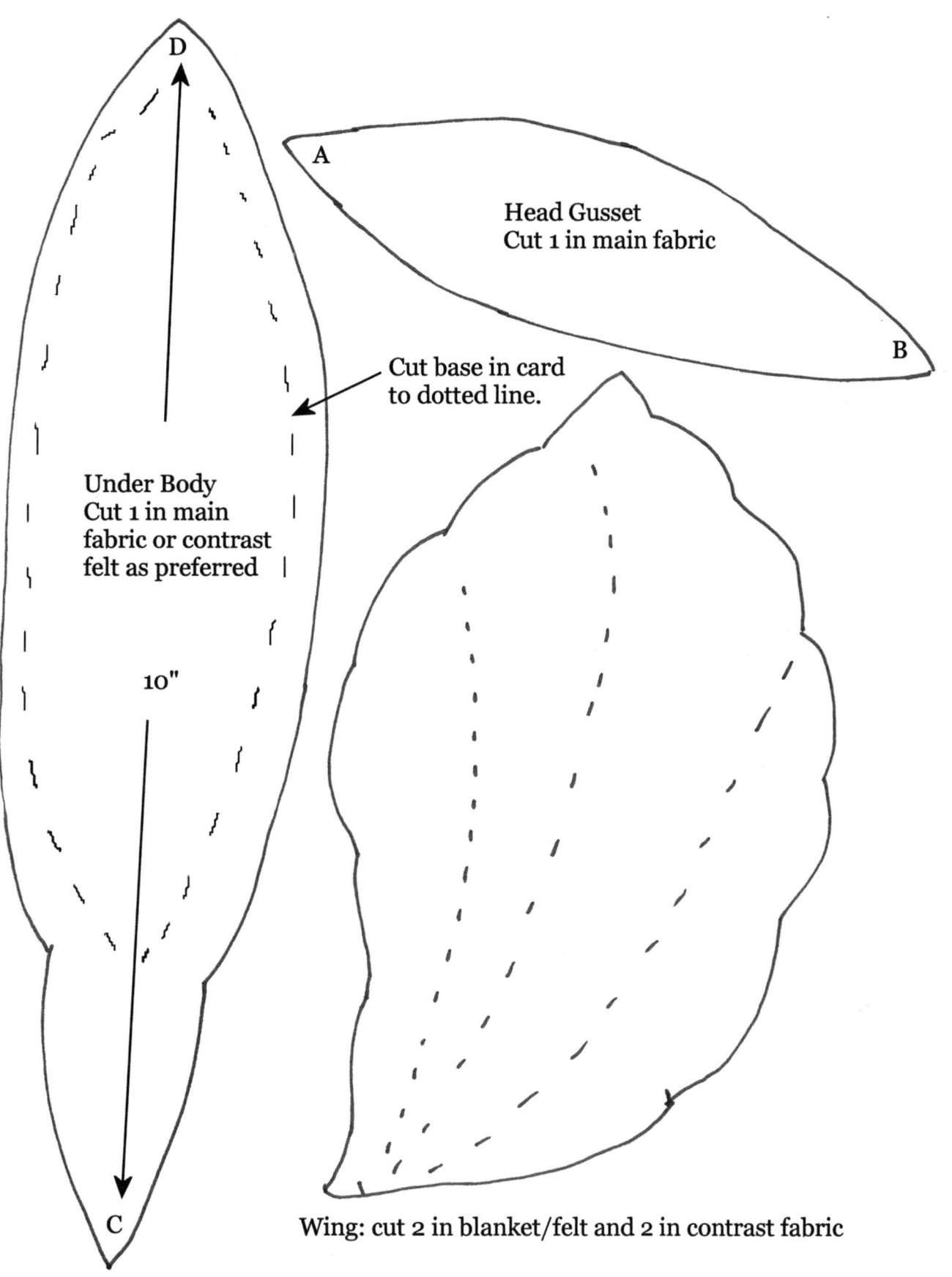

D

A

Head Gusset
Cut 1 in main fabric

B

Cut base in card
to dotted line.

Under Body
Cut 1 in main
fabric or contrast
felt as preferred

10"

C

Wing: cut 2 in blanket/felt and 2 in contrast fabric

- To make the beak, join the two upper pieces on the wrong side from G to F using cross stitch as before.

- Put the black and orange pieces of the under-beak together and stitch all round with running stitch and 2 strands of orange floss.

- Now join upper beak to under beak, with running stitch, matching the letters shown on the template.

- Note: the orange part of the lower beak is on the outside and black on the inside. This makes a clear dividing line where the beak would open in a real swan and adds a lot of character.

- Stuff the beak firmly and sew to the head with small stitches. You will probably find it easiest to use a curved needle for this. Note the positioning and angle of the beak as shown in the photo on the right.

- Take a couple of small stitches at the top of the black part of the beak just above the fold - to make a little tuck in the black felt.

- Attach to head with black floss and curved needle using the photo below as a guide.

- Make up the wings as for the body, then stuff very lightly. Indicate feathers by stitching running stitch lines as shown on the template.

- Attach wings to body as shown in the photo on the left, aligning the bottoms of the wings with the base seam of the body.

- Add your two 1" buttons at the base of the wings as shown. Using your long needle stitch right through the body and pull the buttons tightly against the body - moulding the body shape inwards to make the wings firm and the body nicely rounded.

- Finally attach the two small black beads for eyes. Again pull them firmly against the head so that they sit in two little indentations, giving shape and character to your swan.

FINISHED!!

* A stuffing stick is really handy to push your stuffing up into those hard-to-reach areas. Simply snap the point off a bamboo skewer and "fray" the end slightly so it will grab the stuffing as you push. Easy - but so useful!

18

Diamond Jubilee Quilt: India block

Fabrics from India

Over the centuries India has been renowned as a major producer of rich, vibrant and high quality textiles. Learn a little more about traditional Indian fabrics and how they're made ....

As we begin to consider our Christmas stitching projects, if you're anything like me your thoughts will turn to richly coloured cottons, sumptuous brocades and shimmering silken fabrics, needing only the smallest amount to make your creation feel truly festive. It's likely that some of your Christmassy fabrics originated in India, a country renowned for its rich, vibrant textiles and yarns. Today the country is the second largest producer of fibre in the world, and its textile industry is worth about $55 billion per annum!

Western countries have been importing fabrics from India for centuries - indeed you need only consider the Indian words that have become part of the English language: calico, pyjama, gingham, dungaree, chintz, and khaki to realise how popular and important Indian fabrics have been over the ages. Although most of the fabric production in India is of cotton, Indian silk fabrics are famous for their wonderful vibrant colours and intricate patterns, made possible by complicated dyeing and weaving techniques.

There are traditionally three main methods of decorated fabric production in India - loom weaving and decorating, resist-dyed work (including tie-dyeing, printing and fabric painting techniques) and embroidery. Throughout India, there are regional differences and specialities, for example on the east coast pen-work cloth printers use indigo (easily obtained in the area) and red dyes in their work, but in Gujarat and Rajasthan printers and dyers use both natural and chemical dyes.

Cotton, silk, and wool are the three materials from which textiles are woven. The cotton plant grows in many regions of India, whilst wild silk moths native to the central and north-eastern parts of the country (and different from those found in China) are the source of silk. The fleece of mountain goats from colder regions is spun into wool. Pashmina (also known as cashmere) is made from the fine inner fleece of goats.

The colours most often found in Indian textiles are red, black, blue, violet, green, and yellow and these are obtained from native plants and minerals. Indigo plants are processed and traded in the form of dried cakes that are used to create different shades of blue. Red dye is extracted from trees such as the chai or the madder, and yellow from turmeric or saffron (the latter mostly for silks).

Fabric shop in Delhi, India

Black is created by mixing indigo with an acid substance such as tannin. Green and purple can be made by layering yellow or red dyes over blue cloth. Cotton, unlike silk and wool, must be prepared to receive colour. The fixative agent, known as a mordant, is a metallic oxide that combines with the dye to bond onto the fibre.

Mordants can also be used to create patterns. If the mordant is drawn or stamped with wooden blocks onto the surface of the fabric, the dye adheres only where the substance has been applied and the pattern appears after the cloth has been washed.

Resist dying, also known by the Malay term batik, works in the opposite manner, by using substances such as wax or mud that prevent the dye from bonding to the fabric. After the design elements have been painted or stamped onto the surface of the cloth, it is immersed in a hot dye bath. The shade and depth of the colour is determined by concentration of the dye, duration of the immersion, and number times it is dyed. The final colour will be revealed upon contact with the air.

Patterns are also created by weaving, as is done most often with silks. The term brocade refers to any type of fabric woven with a raised pattern, though usually it indicates that gold or silver thread has been used. Ikats (another Malay term) are cloths whose warp or weft threads have been bound and resist dyed; both sides of the cloth have the same intensity of colour.

Double ikats are cloths in which both warp and weft threads have been bound and resist dyed. When the weft threads are woven onto the loom, they combine with the warp to reveal a pattern of extraordinary density and complexity.

Embroidered fabrics are another Indian speciality, such fabrics often being embellished with beads, shells, mirrors, buttons and sequins. Each caste has its own distinct designs and techniques, which are handed down through the generations. These elaborate embroidered textiles also play an important part in wedding ceremonies and religious festivals, and in some regions of India a bride will take textiles, that she and other women of her family have worked upon, to her husband's home as part of her dowry.

Applique is a relatively recent addition to the tradition of embellished fabrics in India. It's often thought that the technique first appeared in the country in the 19th century, perhaps as a result of contact with Europe or the Middle East through trade. It was usually large friezes or canopies that were appliqued, with mainly figurative designs representing people and animals such as elephants and birds.

Today, Indian textiles remain as popular as ever, and these glorious fabrics are exported worldwide. Instantly recognisable in their wonderful use of colour, Indian fabrics are a high quality product that hold all the vibrancy and energy of their country of origin.

Detail of sari embroidery

sewflapdoodle

Bustle & Sew

Love to Sew and Sew with Love .....

"Trick or Treat? Halloween Fun"

Another of my friend Jacqui's wonderfully simple designs - as she tells me "It's all about the line!" Here the simple stitching is enhanced with a little applique - using vintage fabrics of course!

Pattern shown mounted in 7" hoop.

You will need:

- 9" square cotton or linen or cotton/linen blend fabric in natural colour

- Scraps of fabric in navy blue for hat (black is too harsh), brown/orange and gold for pumpkin

- DMC stranded cotton floss in colours: 310, 553, 726, 761, 823, 838, 841, 946, 975, 3348

- Bondaweb or spray fabric adhesive.

Method:

- Use two strands of floss throughout except for whiskers and eyes.

- Eyes are worked in tiny straight stitches, or you could use a small French knot if you prefer.

- Transfer your pattern to the fabric - the patterns are given actual size to fit within a 7" hoop as shown. I have included a reversed image to suit your preferred method of transfer.

If you are unsure about transferring the design to your fabric, then you will find some hints and tips on doing so on the Free Patterns *page of the Bustle & Sew website.*

- Use your pattern to trace the shapes of the pumpkin and hat onto your Bondaweb (remember this will be reversed). You only need to cut enough yellow fabric for the pumpkin inside (at the back of the rabbit) and to show through the eyes and mouth.

- Apply the yellow fabric first, and then the brown/orange, ironing into place only when you are completely happy with the positioning.

- Secure around the edges with blanket stitch.

- Repeat with the dog's hat, but this time secure around the edges with small straight stitches. I have specified navy blue floss to match the fabric I used, but you may wish to change this to match your own navy fabric. You only need a very tiny amount.

- Stitch the backstitch carefully. This is a very simple stitch - but it isn't always the easiest to make look perfect. Be sure that your needle goes in and out through the same hole and take smaller stitches to fit around curved parts of the design. If in doubt use two shorter stitches rather than one extra long one.

- As Jacqui says "Line is everything" so be very careful to follow your transferred lines exactly. Jacqui's designs are very simple, but if your stitches go astray they just won't look right!

841 back stitch

761 back stitch

838 satin stitch

310 tiny straight stitches

726 blanket stitch

946 blanket stitch

553 back stitch

726 star stitch

823 straight stitch

946 satin stitch

975 back stitch

3348 satin stitch

726 back stitch

23

For the last couple of issues I've been featuring extracts from "The Art and Practice of Mending" by Janie Maud Holt published in 1933 - during times of economic hardship when every penny counted and textile items had to be made to last.

We've taken a look at the (nearly) lost arts of patching and darning, and in this, the final instalment, we're going to be taking a look at mending knitted garments. These skills are very useful to have even today as our increasing reluctance to use harsh chemicals to deal with the constant threat of clothes moths means that even owners of the smartest, best-organised wardrobes may discover unwelcome holes in their favourite woollies when they bring them out of storage for the colder months.

And of course children are always making holes in their favourite knitteds - at least if they're anything like Rosie used to be!

This extract is taken from Chapter VI: Mending Knitted Garments and Stockings

A Thin-Place Darn on Stocking Web.

When hand-knitted garments first show signs of wearing thin, they can be mended most effectively by thin-place darning worked on the wrong side. As

the wool is thick, and also looped, the darn can be made quite invisible on the right side.

Begin working on the wrong side at the left, a little distance from the worn portion. Notice the formation of the knitted stitch with its series of interlocking loops.

Following a straight line of loops, pick up and lay down a row of ascending loops alternately. The darn is made octagonal in shape; the first row of darning stitches should therefore, be the shortest.

Leave a loop at the end of the row, as is usual in darning, and darn downwards, inserting the needle in the row of loops turned downwards one loop higher than the previous row (diagram 40).

Continue darning in the same manner, picking up more loops in each row until the necessary depth of darn is worked; for several rows the edge of the darn may be kept level.

A THIN PLACE DARN ON STOCKING WEB

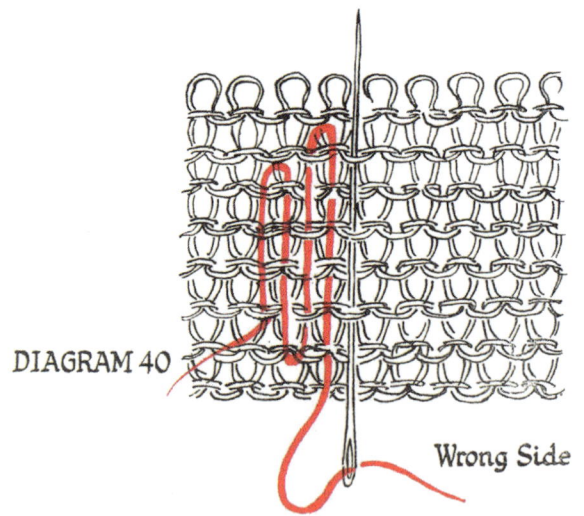

DIAGRAM 40

Wrong Side

Decrease the length of the rows until the darn is of the correct shape and all the worn material is covered.

NOTE: No space is left between the rows of darning as the web is elastic and leaves an adequate distance between the stitches when pulled out.

The Swiss Darn:

The Swiss darn is a type of thin place darning used for repairing knitted garments. As it is a somewhat more difficult method, it is usually reserved for garments of some worth that justify the expenditure of time and trouble. It is particularly useful for garments that have worn thin at the elbows.

In this case work the darning on the right side, following the exact formation of the stitch, so that the new wool is superimposed on the worn loops, covering them completely. For this reason the wool must be an exact match in colour and thickness.

Fasten the end of the wool by running it through the loops for a short distance on the wrong side. Turn the work to the right side and bring the needle out in the centre of a loop A: it is important that the needle should never split a loop of wool in this method of darning.

Now work in a horizontal manner from right to left, inserting the needle in the spaces between two strands of wool B, thus making the first half of a complete loop, and taking the needle back to the original position at A to finish the loop (diagram 41).

The needle and wool are then taken round the strands of wool on a level with A and brought out at C again, making half a loop; when the needle is inserted at B again the loop is completed, and the needle is in position for forming a third loop. Diagrammatically this process looks more complex than it actually is. If the idea is once grasped that the needle and wool follow the formation of the series of loops, each resembling a chain, so that two rows of the knitting are being covered horizontally, very little difficulty will be experienced. This method does take time and is better adapted to coarse hand knitting than to machine-knitted garments made with fine wool.

When the worn part has been covered, turn the work round so that the darning is again being worked from left to right, and proceed to cover two more rows of knitting as before, inserting the needle in the loop last covered by the new wool.

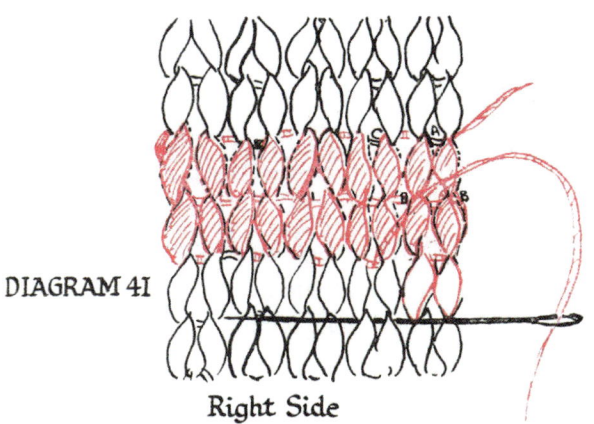

SWISS DARNING OVER A THIN PLACE

DIAGRAM 41

Right Side

The darn when completed should be octagonal in shape and every loop of knitting in the original fabric should be covered with a new loop of darning wool within the area of the darn.

To Mend a Small Hole in Stocking-web

Cut away any worn strands of wool and unravel the knitting until a clear hole is obtained as in the diagram.

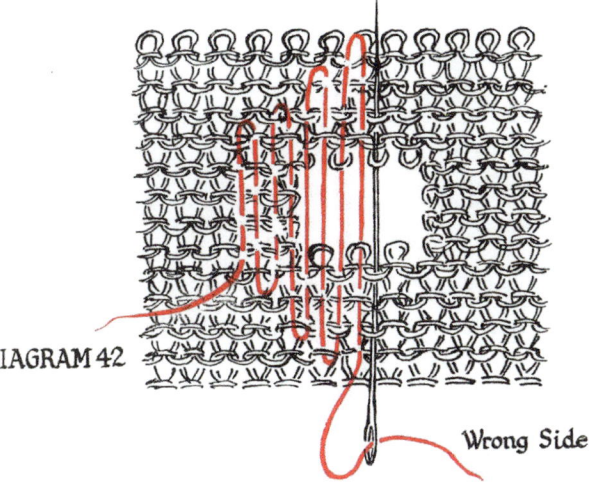

DARN FOR A HOLE IN STOCKING WEB

DIAGRAM 42

Wrong Side

27

Begin at the left hand side and work over the thin material with a thin place darn as described at the beginning of this chapter.

When the hole is reached carry the wool across it, picking up and laying down the edge of the hole, and taking the needle alternately under and over the loops of knitting (diagram 42).

Keep the darn an octagonal shape, and cover all the thin material round the hole.

Turn the work round and begin to work the cross threads about ½ inch from the hole. Pick up and lay down alternate threads as in weaving, and where the darn crosses the knitting pick up and lay down alternate loops.

GRAFTING

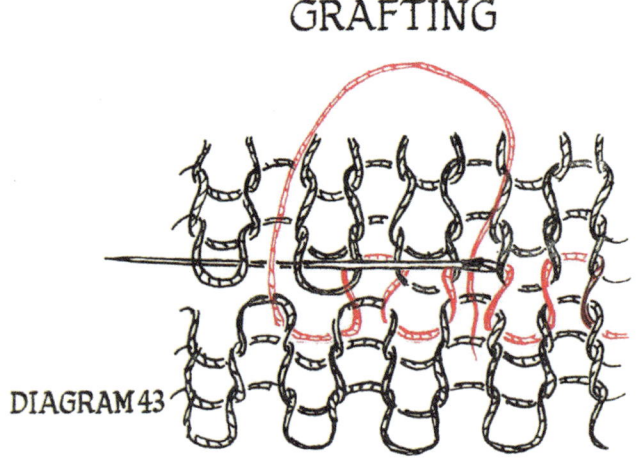

DIAGRAM 43

Grafting

This method of joining two edges of stocking web is used for the darn immediately following the stocking web darn.

It is described first, as the method of inserting the needle in the loops of the knitting is followed throughout the darn, as well as being a means of finishing the darn neatly. As the join made is quite invisible, it is a useful method to employ when making up new garments as well as for mending purposes.

Place the two pieces of stocking web close together with the llops of knitting almost touching one another. If desired the knitting may be tacked on to brown paper, but, on the whole, it is easier to regulate the stitching if it is held firmly between the finger and thumb. Insert the needle through two loops on the bottom row, working from right to left, then carry the wool across to the top edge and inser the needle through two loops there. If a piece of knitting is examined, it will be realised that the loops do not lie exactly opposite one another, a loop lying opposite to a space, and when the needle is inserted through two loops, the thread is carrried one loop forward, first on the top edge and then on the bottom edge (diagram 43).

Continue to insert the needle alternately in the top and bottom edges, as shown in the diagram, until the two pieces are grafted together, and fasten off by running the wool through the back of the knitting for a short distance.

The Stocking-web Darn

This method of darning is suitable for repairing a hole in hand knitted garments such as jumpers, jerseys etc. It is somewhat difficult and is not recommended for garments which will not repay the time expended on them, or for fine woven or knitted fabrics which can satisfactorily be mended in some other way.

The formation of the stocking web is followed as in Swiss darning, but as it is necessary to fill up the hole with new material, some foundation on which to place the loops is required.

Cut away any broken or worn threads, and fray out the hole until the loops of the knitting are plainly visible at each side of the hole.

Using strong thread, connect the loops at each side of the hole by stranding as shown in the diagram, fastening the thread carefully at the beginning and the end (diagram 44).

28

A SWISS DARN ON STOCKING WEB

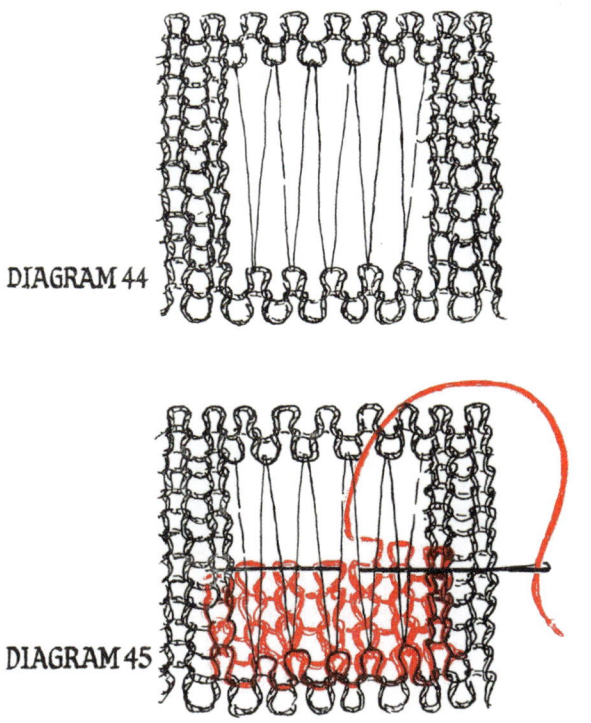

DIAGRAM 44

DIAGRAM 45

Begin working at the bottom of the hole at the right hand side, and cover with a Swiss darn, the loop immediately preceding the one where the stranding begins.

Work across the strands as shown in the diagram, inserting the needle as for grafting in the bottom edge of the darn, and connecting it to the side of the hole when reached.

Turn the work around so that the darn proceeds from right to left, placing new stitches across the strands and inserting the needle into the stitches formed in the previous row (diagram 45).

Care should be taken to ensure that the loops formed are of the same size as those of the main body of the knitting; also that the tension is the same. Puckered or uneven stitches will spoil the appearance of the finished darn.

When the hole is filled, graft the last row of the darn to the top edge of the darn and fasten off neatly. Press beneath a damp cloth.

The wool used for this darn must match exactly the original wool used for the garment, otherwise the darn will not be invisible.

To Mend a Hole by Re-knitting

The following method of replacing the worn part of a knitted garment is more easily and quickly accomplished than a Swiss darn, and for the busy woman will prove a more practicable method.

It is impossible to conceal this mend entirely however.

Cut away all the worn and thin wool and unravel the stitches for a short distance until a clear edge of loops is obtained.

Pick up the stitches on a steel needle and re-knit, using wool that exactly matches the wool of the garment, following the pattern of the knitting.

Graft the new piece to the row of loops at the other edge of the hole, following the method previously described for grafting.

Sew the edges of the new piece of knitting at each side of the hole and press.

Note: If the hole is in an area that experiences extreme or heavy wear, such as an elbow, then coarse black sewing thread knitted in with the new wool will lengthen the wear of the repair.

Repairing knitted garments… re-knitting

Blackbird Patchwork
Cushions

Eagle-eyed readers may well recognise these handsome blackbirds!

Carried away by the ideas of reusing and recycling I decided to slice up and remake the "Love Flew Down at Christmas" cushion I created for the September 2011 issue of this e-zine. So now, instead of one, I have two blackbird cushions, and I managed to fit in all 9 blackbirds too.

Pattern sizes to fit 18" cushion pad.

To make two cushion covers you will need:

- 18" square background fabric - medium weight
- 15" square piece of black felt
- 9 small scraps sparkly fabric, each measuring 2" x 3" approx.
- 9 ¼" cream or mother of pearl buttons
- Gold thread suitable for your sewing machine
- Bondaweb or spray fabric adhesive as preferred
- Non-permanent fabric marker
- Embroidery/darning foot for your machine
- DMC embroidery floss in colours: 310, 321, 347, 407, 470, 471, 581, 729, 801, 937, 970, 3722, 3726, 3823, E5200

- For the log cabin patchwork: an assortment of fabric scraps all at least 2 ½" wide, and the largest 10" in length
- For the simple patchwork: four x 6" squares fabric

- 2 pieces of old blanket each measuring 18" square for backing and quilting front panels (I like to use blanket as this means you don't need a third layer of fabric - the blanket won't break up. If you use quilting batting, then you will also need 18" square backing fabric for each cushion panel)
- 4 rectangles of medium weight fabric each measuring 12" x 18" for the backs of the cushion covers.

NOTE: ¼" seam allowance throughout

First stitch your blackbirds:

Stitch them all onto one piece of fabric, then cut them into 6" squares at the end - this is much easier and less wasteful than trying to hoop up small squares of fabric.

- Fold your fabric into three lengthways and then crossways, pressing on the folds lightly with your hand. Then open it out and you will have nine equal-sized squares. This will help you position your blackbirds. Mark these squares with your temporary fabric marker to help you position your blackbirds.

- Using the template at the end of the pattern, cut out your blackbirds and position them on your background fabric. Place them towards the centre of the squares to allow for seam allowances.

- When you're happy with their positioning, secure in place using either Bondaweb or fabric adhesive, whichever you prefer.

- With gold thread in your machine needle, and your darning foot machine twice around the edges of each blackbird. This is supposed to be slightly "scribbly-looking" so don't make it too neat. Stitch "V" shapes at the tails to represent tail feathers (see photographs for guide).

- Cut out nine wings from your sparkly fabric (remember to reverse one wing) and apply in the same way.

- Transfer the embroidery patterns to your main fabric - they are all very simple so you might find the easiest way is simply to draw them on with your non-permanent pen using the template as a guide. The template is given as actual size. Draw in the blackbirds' legs.

- Stitch the leaves and berries, blackbirds' legs and beaks. Use 3 strands of floss throughout, except for the ladybird which is worked in a single strand of floss. The leaves, stalks and wriggly worm are worked in stem stitch, whilst the berries and rose hips are worked in satin stitch. The centre of the daisy is French knots.

- Secure the buttons for eyes using black floss, and stitch around them in 729 and back stitch. Use 729 for the beaks and legs.

- Press lightly on reverse and then cut into nine 6" squares along the lines you drew.

Log Cabin Patchwork Panel

- From your fabric scraps cut::
  Four 6" x 2 ½" rectangles
  Eight 8" x 2 ½" rectangles
  Four 10" x 2 ½" rectangles

- Choose the four blackbirds you'd like for this cushion and make up 4 log cabin squares, then join the squares into 1 large panel for your cushion front.

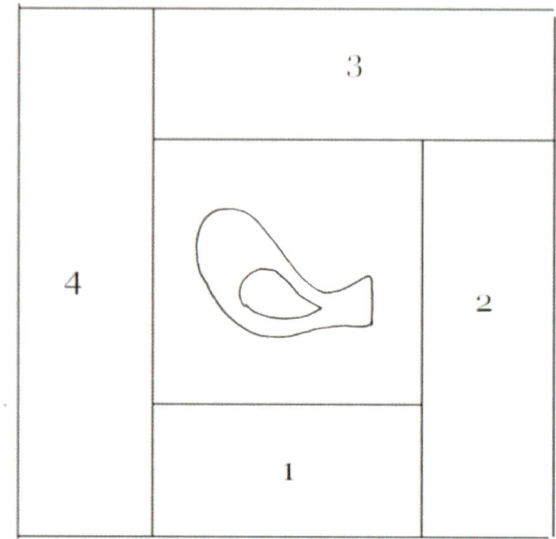

- Place your cushion panel on top of one of your blanket squares (or make a quilting sandwich if using batting) right side up and tack or baste together.
- With your darning foot, stitch in the ditch around the blackbird squares, then stipple all over the rest of the panel (I used green thread as this worked nicely with my fabric choices)
- This panel is now finished.

Simple Patchwork Panel:

- Arrange your blackbird and fabric squares in a 3 x 3 square as shown in the photographs.
- Join them in three strips of three - then join the strips together.
- Press on the reverse.
- Place your cushion panel on top of one of your blanket squares (or make a quilting sandwich if using batting) right side up and tack or baste together.
- With your darning foot, stitch in the ditch around the blackbird squares, then work wavy lines over the fabric squares - again using a contrasting thread is nice.
- This panel is now finished.

Note: Eagle-eyed readers may notice that the images my cushions don't exactly coincide with the directions I've given here. I added extra strips at the centre of the log cabin panel and a border around the simple patchwork panel. This is because I actually cut up last year's cushion and because of the way the blackbirds were arranged I was unable to cut exact squares - this meant some adjustments were needed!

Make and Assemble Covers:

- Take your four 12" x 18" rectangles and hem one of the 18" edges on each panel.
- Place your front panel face up on a clean flat surface.
- Place your reverse panels face down on top of the front panel, matching the unfinished 18" edges to the sides of your front panel. They will overlap by between 4" and 5" at the centre to form your envelope closure.
- Pin and/or tack around edges, then machine stitch around edges - I usually go around twice for extra strength.
- Trim raw edges with pinking shears - or over stitch if prefered and clip corners.
- Turn right side out and press lightly if needed.
- Insert your cushion pads.
- Finished!

"Love Flew Down at Christmas Panel"

Handmade to Sell - Review

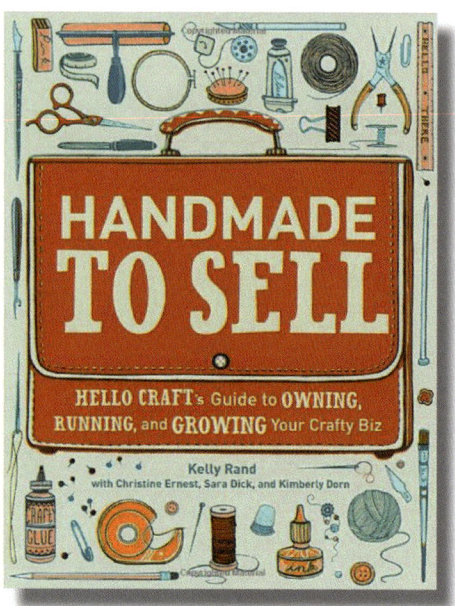

From time to time various publishing companies send me books to review. They are usually expensive-looking hardback books with lots of colourful illustrations and exciting ideas for projects. So when this little paperback book dropped through my letterbox I was underwhelmed to say the least.

All that changed though, once I opened it and started to read. It is 176 pages of really REALLY useful information with stuff I wish I'd known when I first started to craft to sell - too many years ago to remember now!

Of course in the days when I used to craft between Rosie's naps the internet didn't exist, and I used to sell my creations at local craft fairs and markets.

This book covers all you need to know about choosing your craft fair, applying, setting up and more, but that's just one chapter! You'll also find information on business administration, selling online, marketing, creating brand awareness and also (when you've followed their advice and made lots of money!) expanding and employing staff!

My only (slight) problem as a UK based reader is that the book is completely biased towards the US, with no links or resources for overseas readers. Having said that though, so much of the advice is well worth reading, it's still worth investing if you are considering making the jump to selling a few of your creations as a hobby to crafting as a full-time business.

I particularly enjoyed the "Why do you Make" list of questions - to help you decide whether you could turn what you currently do for fun and stress relief into a business. The table (reproduced below) breaks down the differences between being a hobbyist and business person - and certainly tells it like it is!

Available from Amazon.

Hobbyist	Businessperson
You create in your spare time.	You create and plan all the time.
You make primarily for yourself or friends and family.	You make primarily to sell to strangers.
You give away your creations.	You can't afford to give away too many of your creations.
You make for stress relief.	Making can be a major stress.
You make to have a creative outlet.	You don't have as much of a creative outlet.
You occasionally sell an item for fun and, possibly, extra cash.	You are selling year round.
You cannot deduct materials, trainings, and supplies from your taxes.	You can deduct materials, trainings, and supplies from your taxes.

Star of Wonder

A Rosie & Bear Design

Rosie and Bear are sitting on the old window-seat gazing up at the clear starry sky - perhaps they're hoping to spot Santa and Rudolph making their Christmas Eve deliveries?!

Shown mounted in a 6" hoop.

You will need:

- 8" square neutral coloured cotton, linen or cotton/linen blend fabric suitable for embroidery
- DMC stranded cotton floss in colours: 310, 315, 433, 504, 561, 676, 680, 826, 989, 3774, 3845, 3862, 4065, E168, blanc

Notes on working:

- Use two strands of floss throughout.

- Bear's eye and nose are worked in 310 (black floss) with the tiniest little stitch of white to give his eye a bit of sparkle.

- Stars are worked in star stitch in E168

- If you haven't stitched Bear before - then don't worry, fur is really easy when you know how. Just download my free guide "How to Embroider Fur" for all the help you'll need to make your Bear look really furry!

Stitch Guide:

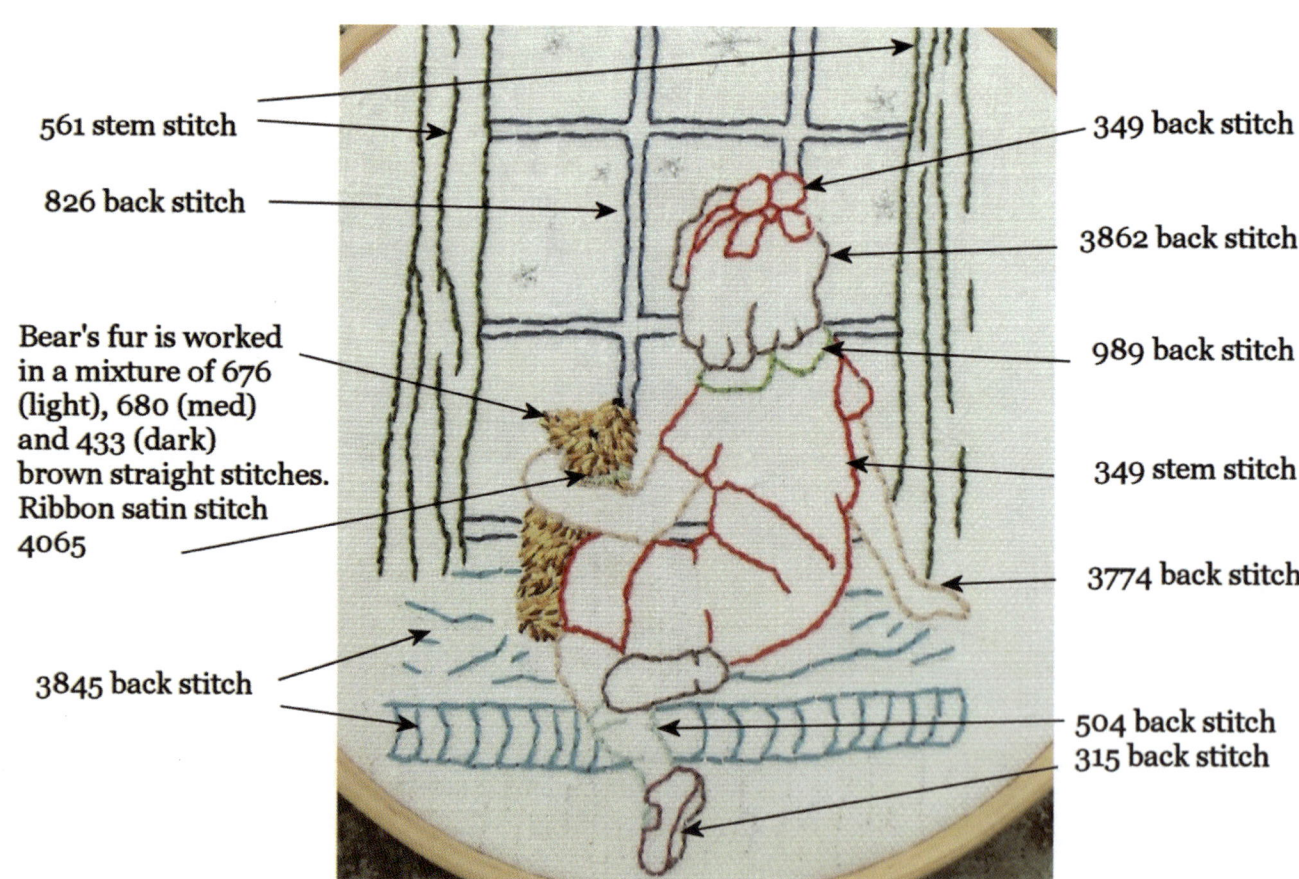

561 stem stitch

826 back stitch

Bear's fur is worked in a mixture of 676 (light), 680 (med) and 433 (dark) brown straight stitches. Ribbon satin stitch 4065

3845 back stitch

349 back stitch

3862 back stitch

989 back stitch

349 stem stitch

3774 back stitch

504 back stitch
315 back stitch

Pipany & the Poltisko Memoirs.

My website address: www.pipany.co.uk

This month I am delighted to be able to bring you an interview with the nimble-fingered and amazingly talented Cornish designer-maker, Pipany.

I have been a great admirer of her work for a very long time - and am extremely jealous of her wonderful photography skills as she manages to turn even the most every-day scenes and objects into delightful images, with never a wonky horizon or black furry tail in sight!

Like me, Pipany lives on the coast, though she lives in Cornwall, and her blog is full of her family's adventures in that delightful part of England. She offers a delightful range of hand-stitched items for sale - so if you're a bit daunted by the amount of stitching you still have left for Christmas, then you could always consider "cheating" and visit her website for some lovely unique gifts.

A trio of Babbits!

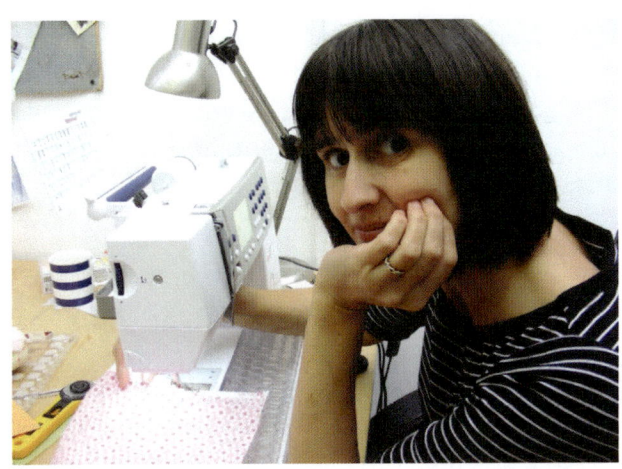

Hi Pipany, and thanks for joining us. I'd like to start by asking if you could tell us a little about yourself and when you learned to sew?

Hello and thank you so much for making me a part of this month's issue.

I am lucky enough to live in beautiful Cornwall with my lovely partner Dave and our rather large family of seven children ranging in age from 29 to 6 years old. Though the older ones no longer live at home they do return very frequently for large gatherings which get very noisy!

We also have a growing menagerie of hens, ducks, cats, guinea pigs and a rabbit; a beautiful, rather natural garden where we grow flowers to cut for the house, herbs & vegetables and a fair amount of fruit. There is always something going on.

Like so many designer-makers I have created for as long as I can remember. Whether it was making dolls house furniture out of matchboxes and fabric scraps, sketching or gardening with my Dad ,I was usually to be found somewhere busily involved in something of a practical nature. I also loved (and still do) the escapism reading offered. In fact, really I have always been drawn to anything creative.

Have you had any formal design training?

I have never had any formal training, merely a have-a-go attitude and a determination to learn. I taught myself to crochet when I was quite small by reading books - no internet back then - and once I had learnt a few basics I went straight on to crocheting a shawl for my Mum. She was really my inspiration having taught me and my six sisters to knit at a very young age and showing me how to embroider.

One of my favourite things is the little hand embroidered picture she made years ago of a cottage garden with its beautiful hollyhocks of French knots and lazy daisy chrysanthemums. I think it is much easier to learn any craft these days with so many great online tutorials around. It's the practice that hones the basics.

How/why/when did your business begin?

In 2006 I was at home with our youngest daughter, Isabella, who was only at the time about 3 months old. I knew that if I didn't take the chance then to have a go at building a business then I probably never would, so with no experience whatsoever Dave and I built a website using Moonfruit.com, a self-build package which I cannot recommend highly enough.

It took the whole of the summer holidays but by mid-September it was ready to go live with around six products I had designed, made and photographed. It was so very exciting and more than a little scary too.

I learnt so much in those early years; everything from photography, product copy, packaging, website maintenance, etc was suddenly all I could think about and certainly all I ever talked about. I must have been a joy to live with!

Gradually I built up an online presence through my blog Pipany & the Poltisko Memoirs where I chat about my daily life in Cornwall.

One day I may be writing about sailing our little boat Mermaid along the River Fal, the next describing a foraging session in the lanes where we may have picked a batch of blackberries to turn into wine. I also use the blog to talk about the business whether showcasing new products or discussing a problem I have encountered. I know I like to hear the ups and downs of business life and I think that seems to be true of my readers.

I love your tales of family life, and your wonderful photography over on your blog - how do you manage to organise your time to fit in stitching and designing too? Is there such a thing as a typical day for you?

Mostly I am incredibly strict about my working day which begins straight after the school run. Dave converted the back half of our double garage into a studio for me and from the moment I get back from dropping the children off till the moment I have to fetch them I try not to touch any housework. If I allowed myself to drift around the house I would never be able to keep up with orders or admin.

The hardest part is the after school bit when all I want to do is either collapse in a chair or carry on with a project that has really gone well that day, but all the other tasks are waiting for me just like everyone else.

I suppose the thing I find hardest to make time for is designing which is actually my favourite. There is always so much else that feels more pressing but at the same time it is important to keep things fresh.

As for the family side of things, I am very lucky in that we have so much fun as a family. We love to play board games together or chill our around the fire with a good film. As I said before, the older ones pop home often and we even have a little grand-daughter now which is just lovely.

At Christmas I get everyone involved with cutting out fabric or packaging orders and then we'll all gather round the the table for a huge meal. It all sounds a bit like The Waltons but there are plenty of squabbles to keep things real!

How do you find inspiration for your designs?

My main design inspiration is my home and the things we do here. For instance, my Berry range of products came about as I picked the redcurrants from the garden in the summer. The scarlet globes just shone at me like jewels and I instantly stopped what I was doing to grab my camera so I had a reference point once I was back indoors.

The design just drew itself really and the touch of Cornish Blue applique happened as I sipped tea from one of our cups. Other things that inspire me are the amazing Cornish landscape. I love this county with all my heart and am constantly inspired by the things I see daily.

Seeds and grasses appeared as part of a range of covered journals and cushions after a particularly bountiful autumn walk. The best way to be inspired is to get outdoors and just look around you. There will always be something.

What are your favourite fabrics and threads to work with, and do you find these change over time - or perhaps with the seasons around you?

My favourite fabrics to use are probably the gorgeous linen-cotton fabric I use as a background for most of my products. It has a lovely feel and that gorgeous slubiness you only seem to get with a linen mix.

I also love the brighter fabrics I used for my Lauren Tote Bags and change these every few years to enable me to have a legitimate excuse for fabric

43

shopping! My favourites for these come from Prestigious Fabrics. Really though I just love fabric, any fabric!

Lauren Tote Bag

Do you have a favourite pattern (mine is your Babbits and their stories!)

Well yes, those Babbits have taken on a real life of their own! They do have a soft spot with me as I originally designed one for my daughter Lucy and the name Babbit came about because Isabella couldn't actually say rabbit! The name Babbit stuck and now we have tales of the various ones I have made as they travel all over the world.

It makes me feel very special that these little guys have become so popular and they do look funny lined up on my sewing room shelves!

I also am really pleased with my Personalised Berry Lavender Cushion which is filled with lavender from our garden. I like to think of the fact that the design not only originated in Cornwall, but in my very own garden.

Do you have any new products in mind for Christmas?

Yes I do. As well as my Mistletoe and Noel embroidered Heart decorations which are always very popular I am just putting the finishing touches to some new designs for Christmas which will have a slight seaside feel to them - a sort of Cornish Christmas I suppose.

I also have some new gift products which will be out soon including a range which can be personalised to make them even more special. These will include a little bag for a girl and some new journal designs. Watch this space!

Thank you Pipany - and you can keep up to date with all the goings-on in Cornwall on Pipany's blog:

http://www.pipany-poltiskofarm.blogspot.co.uk/

and see her full range of products on her website:

http://pipany.co.uk

"I Saw Three Ships" Table Runner

This is a wonderful pattern for using up all those tiny scraps of fabric - and for turning not very much indeed into a unique Christmas work of art - sure to be treasured and brought out year after year!

Finished size 50" x 18" (approx)

You will need:

- 30 x 5" squares festive fabrics for the patchwork border (*I used a Moda charm pack: Dear Mr Claus by Cosmo Cricket*)
- 32" x 12" cream medium weight fabric for background (quilting weight will not be strong enough to take all the machine embroidery/applique)
- 52" x 20" medium weight fabric for backing
- 32" x 4" strip of dark blue fabric for sea
- Lots of scraps of felt, fabrics and some ric rac braid to create your applique picture.
- Stranded cotton floss in light gold-brown, brown, black, pink and gold
- Bondaweb and temporary fabric adhesive
- Temporary fabric marker pen
- Embroidery/darning foot for your machine
- Black and cream thread for your machine

Applique Panel:

This is huge fun to create. There's nothing particularly difficult about it - simply stick your pieces down and stitch ... but there are lots of layers and some of the pieces are quite small, so I would recommend setting aside some clear time to concentrate on one ship at a time to make sure that, for example, you don't suddenly discover you've stuck down an angel's head without first applying the halo behind it!

If you're not sure about this technique, then you might find my video tutorials useful:

CLICK HERE FOR PART ONE

CLICK HERE FOR PART TWO

- Take your cream fabric and fold the two short edges together to find the centre point. Measure 2" up from the bottom edge and mark this point. This will be the position of the centre of the bottom edge of your middle ship (Mary and Jesus).

- Using the templates (they are given at 75% of actual size) at the end of the pattern, trace the ship body and sail onto your bondaweb and fuse to the back of the fabric you have chosen for these shapes. Cut out the shapes but do not remove the Bondaweb at this point. (from now on I will assume you will always trace and fuse the Bondaweb before cutting out your shapes).

- Now cut out and position your shapes for Jesus and Mary - keep checking they fit correctly into the ship by placing your ship sail and body around them as you work

- Note: work from the back forwards - so position your halo first - cutting a little extra so it will underlap the heads, then the heads, with slightly longer necks to underlap the bodies. This avoids any awkward joins or ugly gaps.

- When you're happy with the positioning remove Bondaweb and fuse into place.

- Position your ship body and sail shapes and fuse into place.

- Then the trims and decorations on the ship - be sure to fuse the ends of the ric-rac braid beneath the fabric rectangles at either end of the ship.

- Draw in the lines for the mast and rigging with your temporary fabric marker pen.
- Machine stitch around the edges of your shapes, going around twice (except for figures) and aiming for a scribbled effect.
- Machine stitch the rigging. DO NOT stitch the mast and spar at the front of the ship - you will hand embroider these

- Then hand stitch the mast (using parallel rows of chain stitch and dark brown) and the spar (chain stitch and light golden brown). Stitch the figures' hair. Add rosy cheeks and little black eyes

- Repeat these stages with the other two ships. The ships are positioned 3" apart and there are close up photos of the appliques on the next pages to follow.
- The angel in the first ship is blowing a trumpet - I added some musical notes in black floss to my design.
- When your ship appliques are complete, cut a wavy edge along the top of your dark blue fabric and position to cover the bottom edges of the ships. You might also like to add some green felt shapes as extra waves.
- When happy with your sea, stitch into place. (you could add some fish too, if you wanted!)

Assemble your table runner:

- When your applique is finished press lightly on the reverse

- Take your 5" squares and arrange them around the edge of your applique to decide upon the layout you would like - there will be 7 along the top and bottom of your panel and two and blocks of 8 at each side.

- *Note: all seam allowances are ¼"*

- Join the bottom 7 squares into a strip and using the stitch and flip technique sew them to your applique panel. Position the strip so that just a small amount of sea is showing.

- When you've stitched this strip, then trim away any excess applique fabric to ¼"

- Sew your squares into 2 blocks of 3 x 2 for the sides, then stitch to your applique in the same way, trimming away excess applique fabric.

- Finally add your top 11 squares as a single strip so you've created your patchwork border for your table runner.

- Place your backing fabric and panel right sides together and stitch around the edges, leaving a 6" gap for turning.

- Clip corners and turn right side out. Press, then top stitch around edges ¼" from edge, including over your turning gap.

- Press again - FINISHED!!

49

Rosie's Recipes

Song of The Witches by William Shakespeare

Double, double toil and trouble;

Fire burn and caldron bubble.

Fillet of a fenny snake,

In the caldron boil and bake;

Eye of newt and toe of frog,

Wool of bat and tongue of dog,

Adder's fork and blind-worm's sting,

Lizard's leg and howlet's wing,

For a charm of powerful trouble,

Like a hell-broth boil and bubble.

Double, double toil and trouble;

Fire burn and caldron bubble.

Cool it with a baboon's blood,

Then the charm is firm and good.

Halloween is almost here, so this month I have chosen some of my favourite Halloween themed recipes. I love fancy dress and

Halloween is the perfect opportunity to dress up. When I was younger mum made me a spectacular spider web costume for a friend's Halloween Party. She made the body of the costume out of a sheet and painstakingly sewed on sequins to create a sparkly black web. There was also a spider in the middle, surrounded by little flies that had become tangled in his web. Now I am older my Halloween costumes are not so elaborate, although I always make sure to dig out the cat ears and draw on some whiskers ready for any trick or treaters that knock on my door.

Whether you love it or hate it, you can be sure to hear a chorus of 'trick or treat' this all All Hallows Eve.

Scary Spider Cupcakes

Ingredients:

For the sponge:
3 eggs
200g caster sugar 200g
self-raising flour 200g
butter, melted 100g
cocoa powder

For the icing:
135g icing sugar
55g butter
30g of sifted cocoa powder

To decorate:
3 liquorice wheels (depending on how long you want the legs to be)
Chocolate sprinkles
Red smarties or M & M's
Black decorative icing (for the eyes)

Method:

o Preheat oven to 180˚ and line a 12 hole muffin tin with paper cases – brown cases work best for the spiders.

o Whisk together the eggs and sugar until light and fluffy.

o Gradually add the flour, cocoa and the melted butter, gently folding the mixture together.

o Pour the mixture evenly into the paper cases.

o Pop in the oven for 10-15 minutes until golden brown.

o Allow to cool for ten minutes on a wire rack before removing from the tin.

o To make the icing, mix together the icing sugar, butter and cocoa powder using an electric whisk

o Top the cakes with the icing (important to be very liberal here!) and sprinkle with chocolate sprinkles.

o Cut lengths of the liquorice for legs and add Smarties for eyes. Add two little blobs of icing for the pupils.

Googly Eyeball Pasta

Ingredients (to make 4 portions):

300g of green Tagliatelle
Mini Mozzarella balls

Pasta sauce
Cherry tomatoes
Basil
Green pesto

Method:

- Cook the Tagliatelle in boiling water for 7-8 minutes

- Gently heat the pasta sauce

- Cut the cherry tomatoes in half and scoop out the insides

- Pop a mini mozzarella ball inside and add a little bit of basil for the pupil

- Add the pesto to the pasta and mix well

- Top with the pasta sauce and add the tomato and mozzarella eyeballs

Chocolate & Toffee Apples

Ingredients:

Toffee Apples

8 apples
400g golden caster sugar
1 tsp vinegar
4 tsp golden syrup

Chocolate Apples

Apples
Milk chocolate

56

Sprinkles or nuts
Wooden skewers/lolly sticks

Method:

o   Place the apples in a large bowl, then cover with boiling water (you may have to do this in 2 batches). This will remove the waxy coating and help the caramel to stick. Dry thoroughly and twist off any stalks. Push a wooden skewer or lolly stick into the stalk end of each apple.

o   Lay out a sheet of baking parchment and make sure it is close to hand.

o   For the toffee apples, tip the sugar into a pan and add the water. Cook over a medium heat for 5 minutes until the sugar dissolves. Stir in the golden syrup and vinegar.

o   Set a sugar thermometer in the pan and boil to 140°C or 'hard crack' stage. If you don't have a thermometer you can test the toffee by pouring a little into a bowl of cold water. It should harden instantly and, when removed, be brittle and easy to break. If you can still squish the toffee, continue to boil it.

o   Carefully dip each apple into the pan and twirl in the toffee until evenly covered. Place on the baking parchment to harden.

o   For the chocolate apples, melt the chocolate in a bowl over a pan of boiling water.

o   Dip the apples into the bowl and twist until covered in chocolate.

o   Sprinkle with nuts or sugar sprinkles and place on the baking parchment to set.

I hope you have enjoyed this month's Rosie's Recipes and have fun making my Halloween recipes.

Rosie x

BUSTLE & SEW

The "Bustle & Sew Magazine" is a Bustle & Sew publication. To see my full range of Rosie & Bear publications, together with many more stitching, applique, softie and quilting projects please visit my website:

www.bustleandsew.com

Bustle & Sew designs

You can also find out about my Bustle & Sew Magazine on my website. This is my monthly e-zine packed with unique projects, articles, features and loads more, and is by far the best (and nicest!) way to build your collection of Bustle & Sew patterns…

You'll never be stuck for ideas again!! Just visit the magazine page on my website to learn more:

www.bustleandsew.com/magazine.

Printed in Great Britain
by Amazon.co.uk, Ltd.,
Marston Gate.